GOD LOVES YOU MOST

By Tara Norbeck

Illustrated by Tori Higa

God Loves You Most
Copyright © 2026 by Tara Norbeck

Library of Congress Cataloging-in-Publication Data

LCCN: 2026902696 (paperback) ISBN: 978-1-961732-35-3 (ebook) | ISBN: 978-1-961732-36-0 (paperback) | ISBN: 978-1-961732-37-7 (hardcover)

Any internet addresses (website, blogs, etc.) and telephone numbers in this book are offered as a resource. They are not intended in any way to be or imply an endorsement from Called Creatives Publishing, nor does Called Creatives Publishing vouch for the content of these sites and numbers for the life of this book.

All rights reserved. No portion of this book may be reproduced or shared in any form – electronic, printed, photocopied, recording, or by any information storage or retrieval system, without prior written permission from the author. The use of short quotations is permitted.

Published in association with Called Creatives Publishing
Gallatin, Tennessee

www.calledcreativespublishing.com

Cover design: Tori Higa
Interior Illustrations: Tori Higa
Interior design: Dallas Hodge

2026 - First Edition

For Avery and Brooke,
who made me a Gigi
and filled my heart with joy!
May you always know
how deeply you are loved—
and that God loves you
most of all.

I LOVE PETTING PLAYFUL PUPPIES.

BUT I LOVE YOU MORE.

BUT I LOVE YOU MORE.

I LOVE BOUNCING WITH BABY BUNNIES.

I LOVE CHASING CHEERFUL CHIPMUNKS.

I LOVE FEEDING FLUFFY FERRETS.

BUT I LOVE YOU MORE.

I LOVE DANCING IN THE DAYLIGHT
WITH DUCKLINGS.

BUT I LOVE YOU MORE.

BUT I LOVE YOU MORE.

NOW YOU KNOW I LOVE YOU MORE.

BUT THERE'S SOMEONE WHOSE LOVE
IS BIGGER THAN ANYONE ELSE'S.

IT'S GOD!

GOD LOVES YOU MOST!

About the Author

Tara Norbeck is a Christ-following wife to John, mom to four, and Gigi. She loves reading, singing, and creating silly stories and songs that point little hearts to Jesus. She and her husband live in Texas. A former Director of Children's Ministries, Tara has seen firsthand the power of simple, God-centered truths in the lives of young children. She believes even the youngest hearts can grasp big, eternal truths, and it is one of her greatest joys to serve God's precious children through story and song, helping them discover the wonder of His love and truth.

To learn more about Tara or to download 7 short bedtime prayers, visit taranorbeck.com or scan the QR code below.

About the Illustrator

Tori Higa is a grown-up who never stopped coloring. She is inspired by God's creation, family & friends, coffee shops, people-watching, and all things vintage. She loves to make art to help point kids to Christ and considers it a high honor to help make books to inspire kids and encourage their faith journey. She currently lives in Southern California with her husband, two teenagers, and a playful little mutt named Edie.
Connect with her @ToriHigaCreates or torihiga.com

www.ingramcontent.com/pod-product-compliance
Ingram Content Group UK Ltd.
Pitfield, Milton Keynes, MK11 3LW, UK
UKHW060124240426

12049UKWH00011B/152